# At a Tip

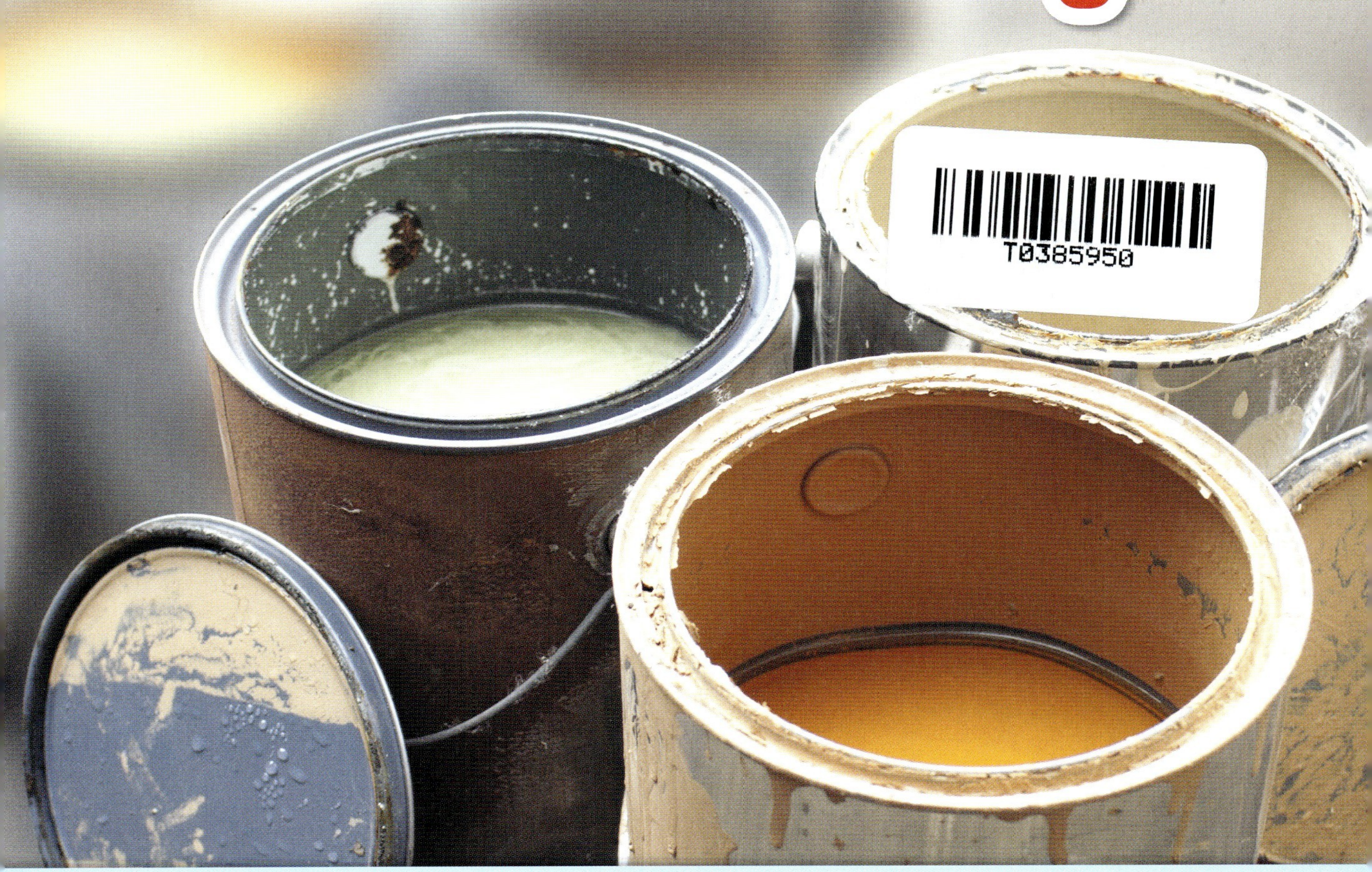



Written by Kathryn Stewart

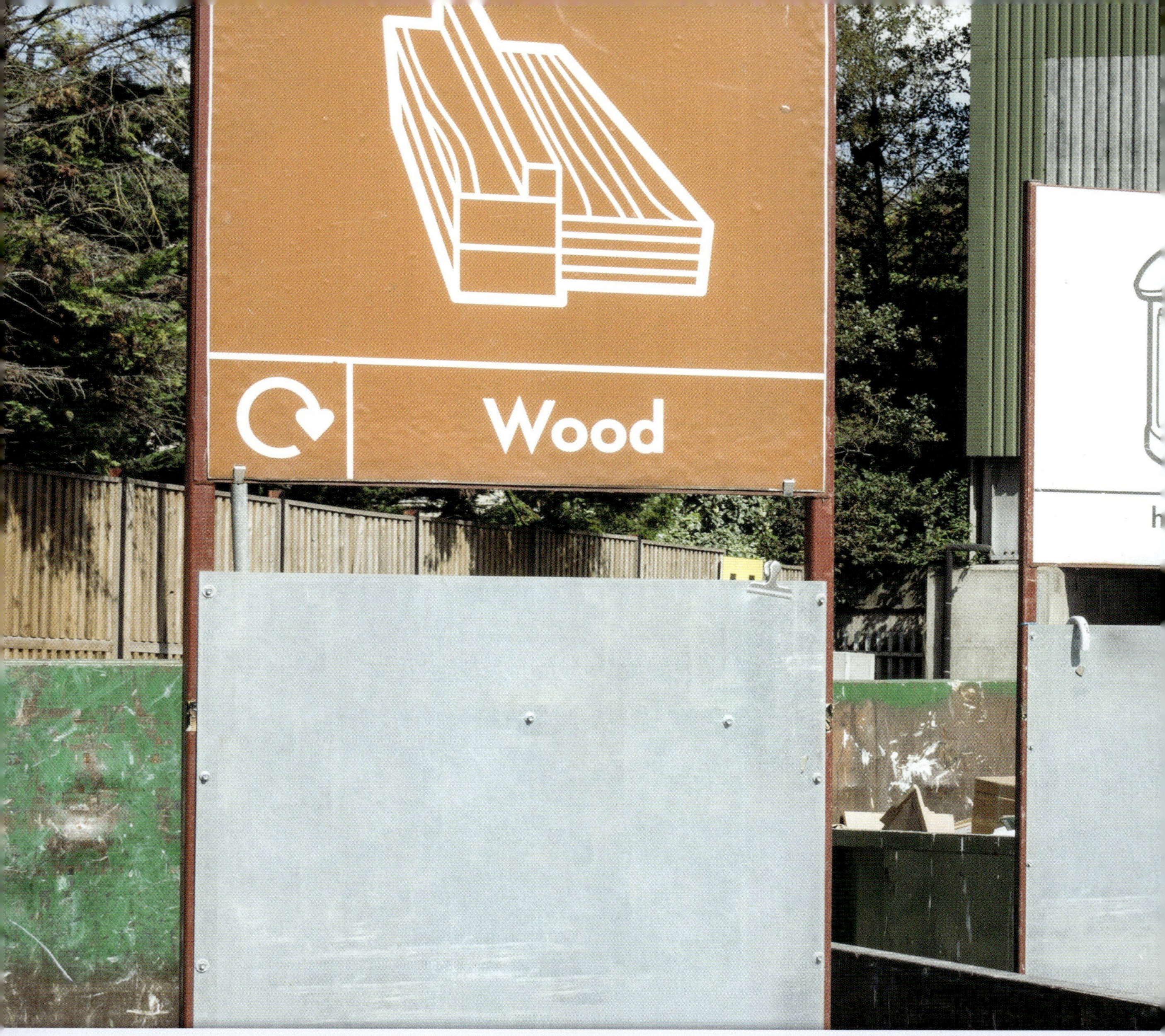


At a tip.

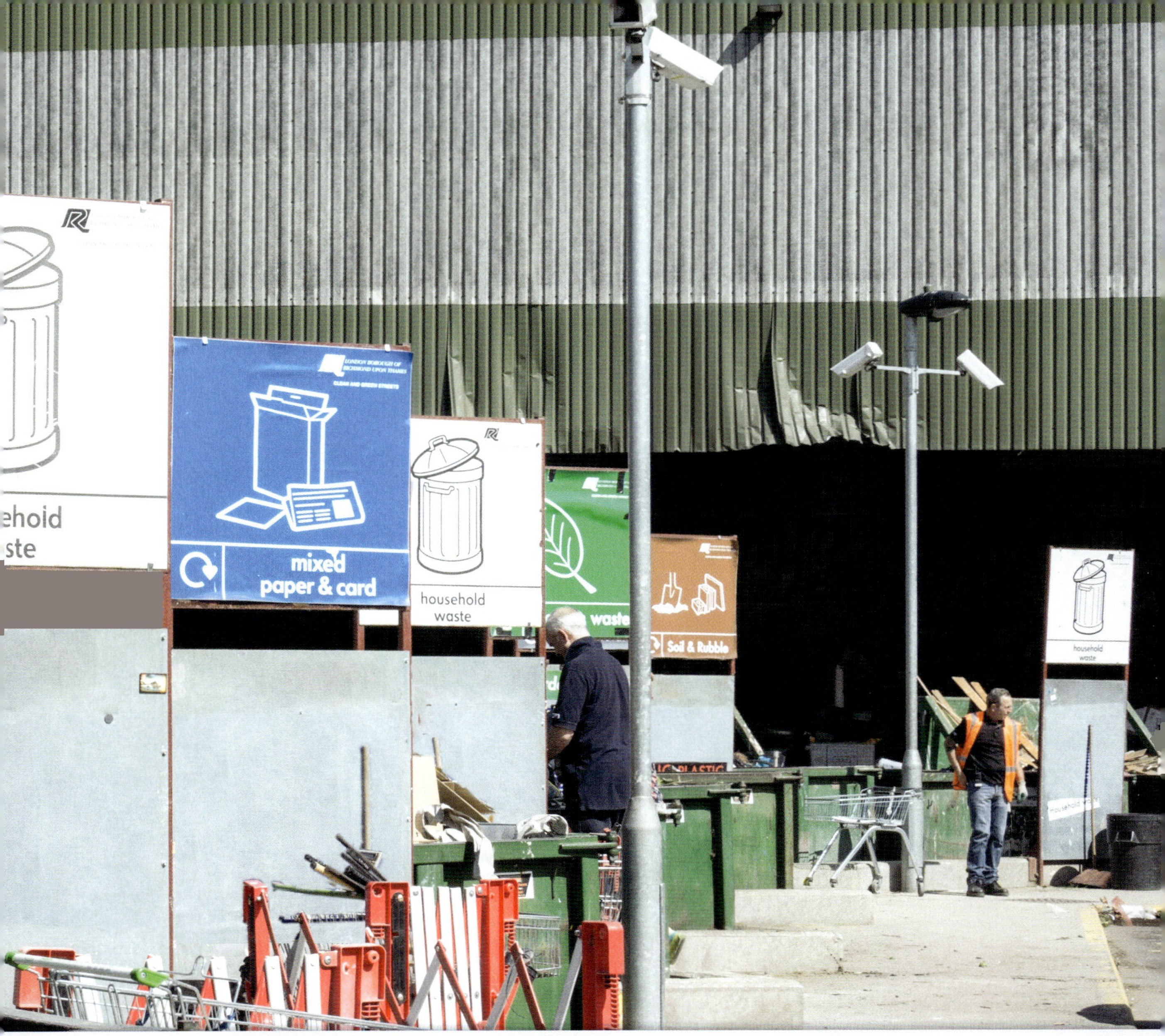
mixed
paper & card
household
waste
waste
Soil & Rubble
household
waste

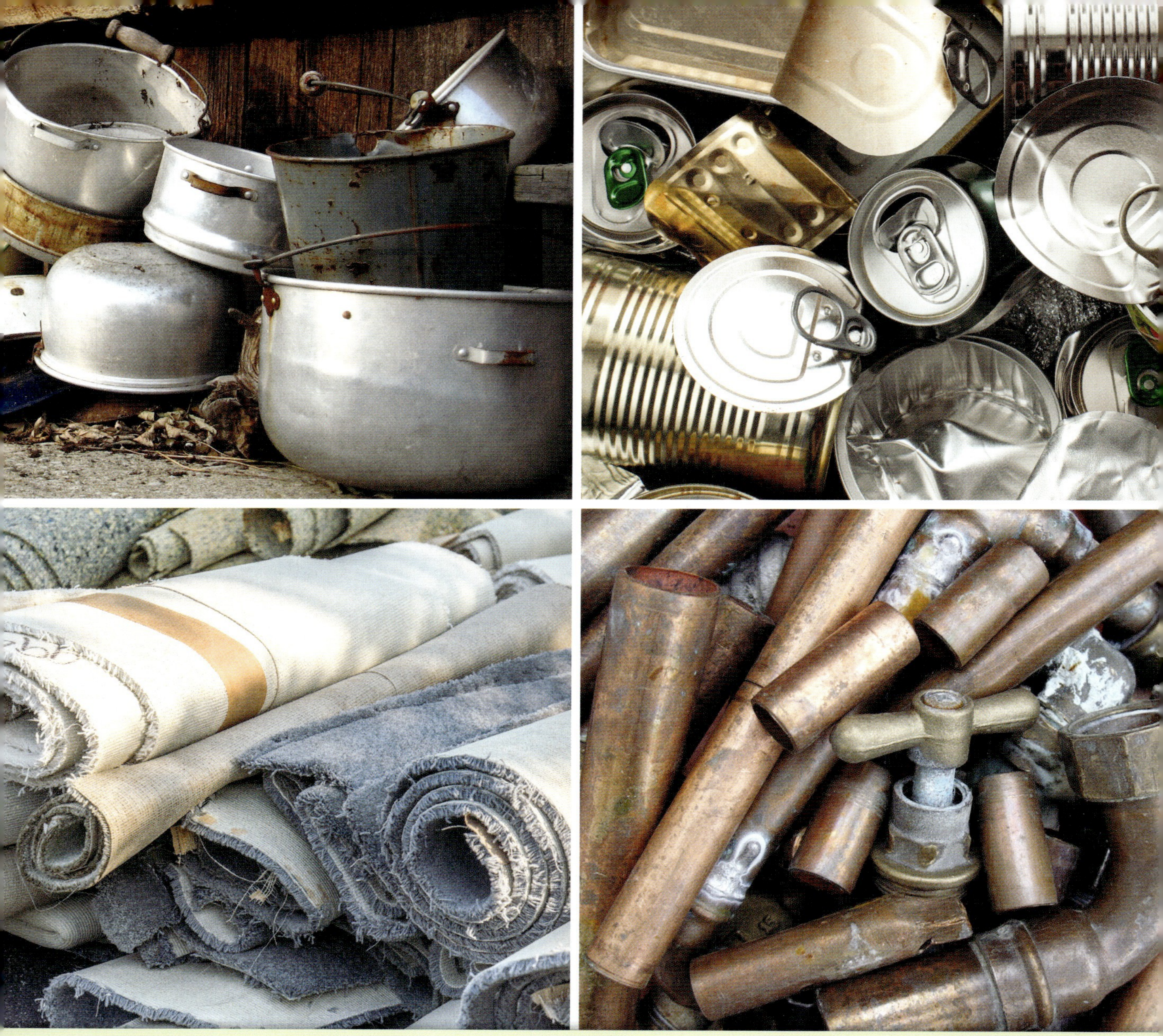

Pans, tins, mats, taps.

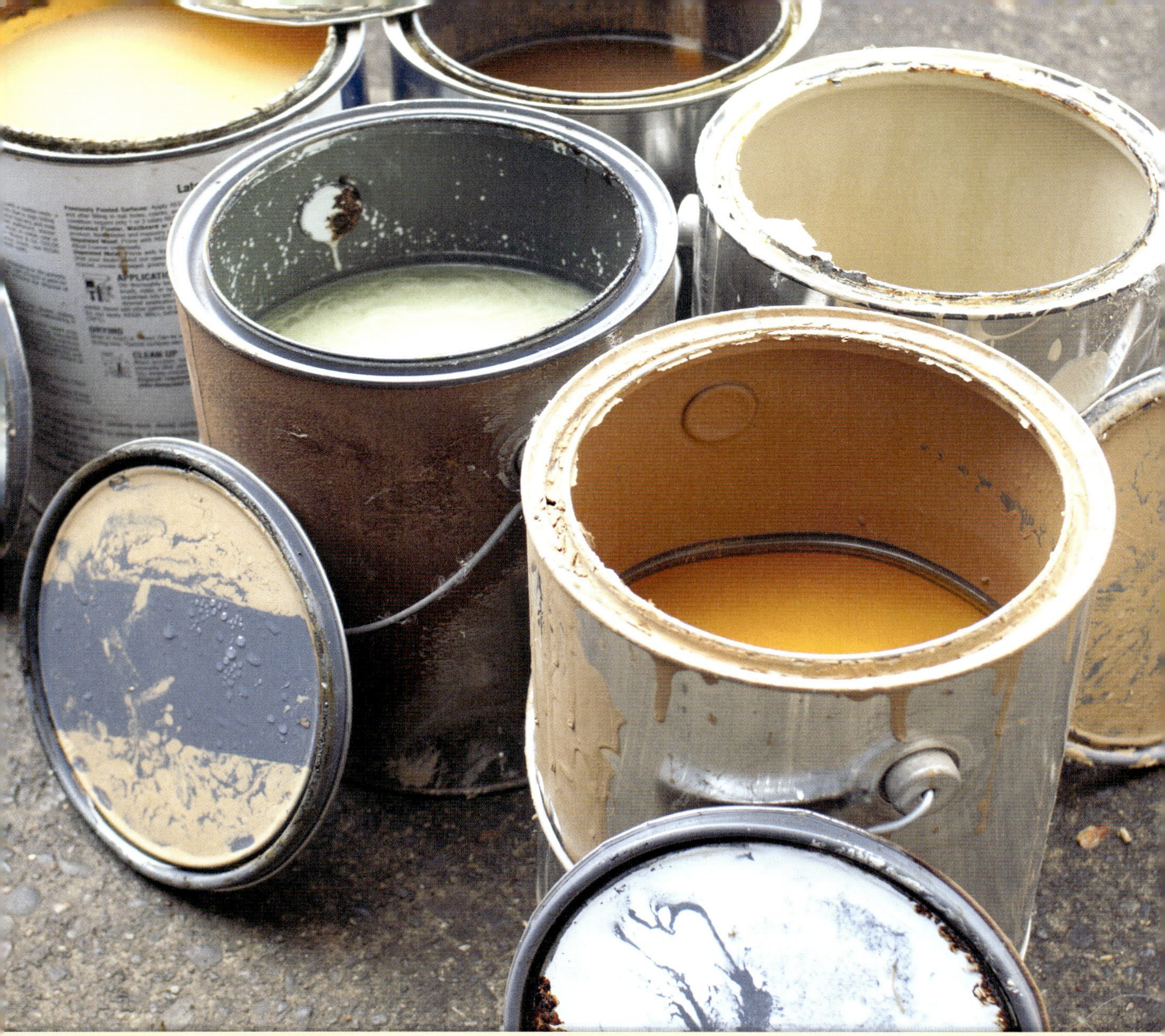

Tins in a tip.

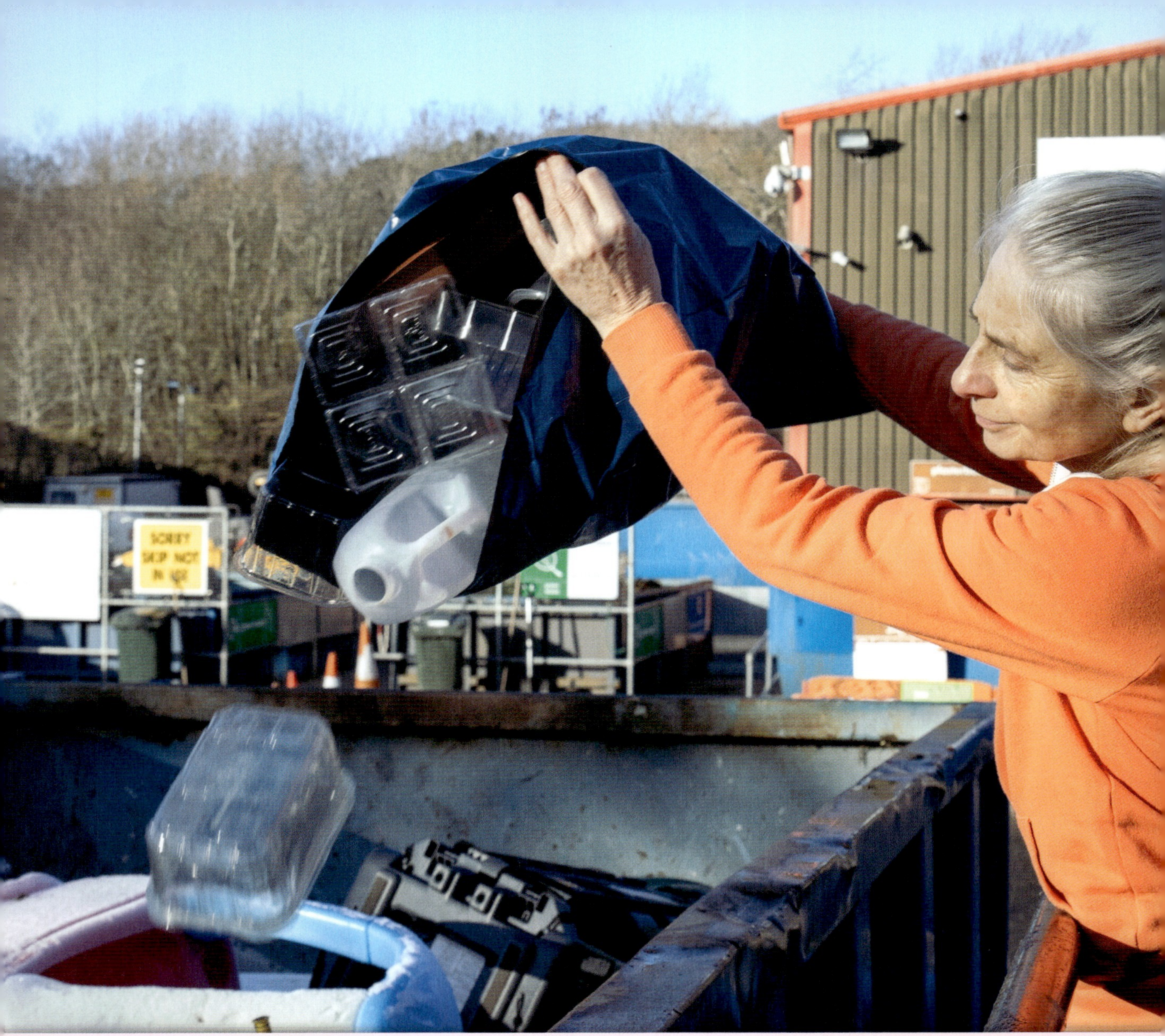

Tip it!

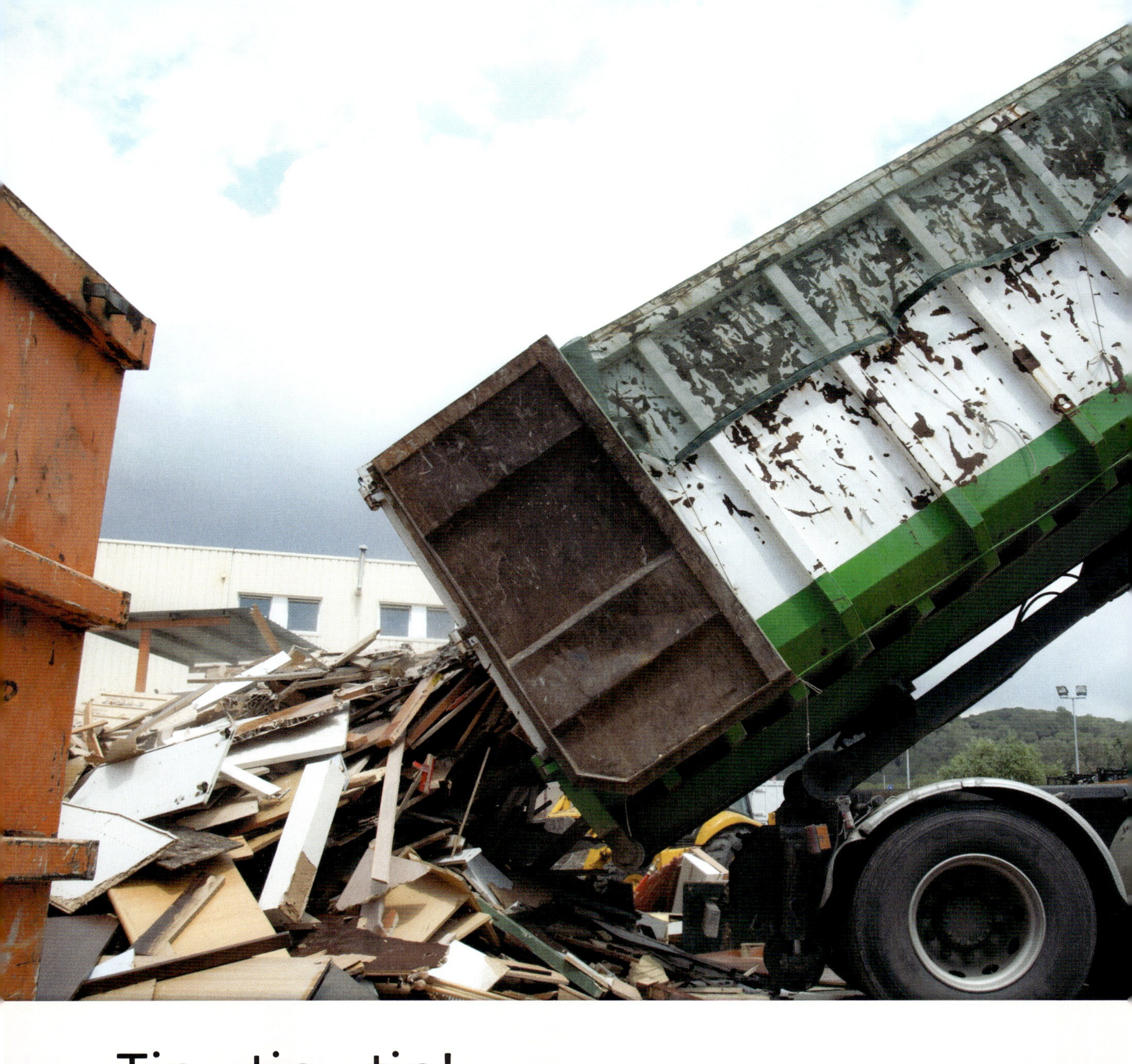

Tip, tip, tip!

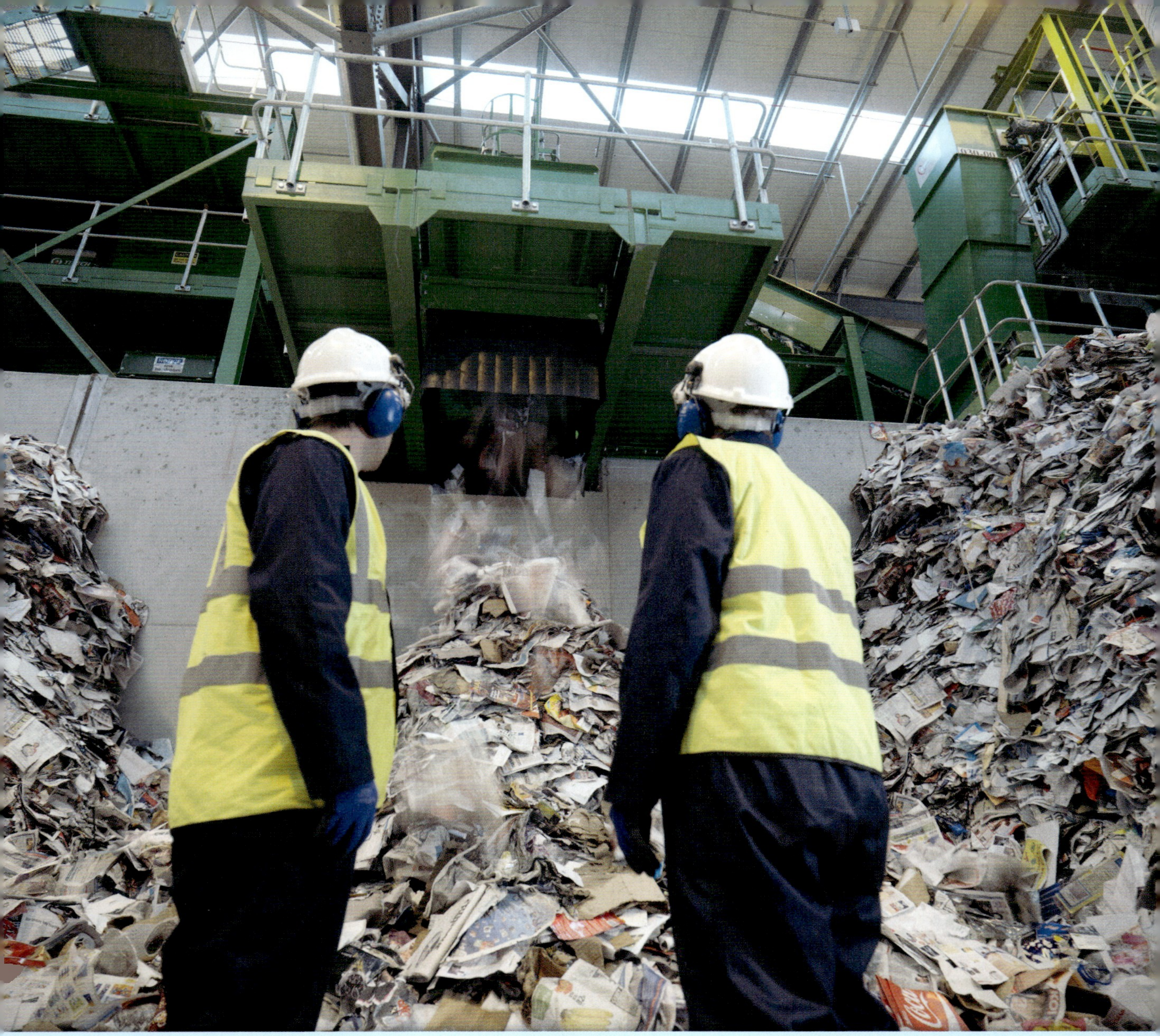

It is a din!